Hangin' with My

A Little Book of
PEEPS® Puns

Illustrated by **MELISSA MATHIESON**

RUNNING PRESS

PHILADELPHIA

Running Press
Hachette Book Group
1290 Avenue of the Americas, New York, NY 10104
www.runningpress.com
@Running_Press

First Edition: January 2025

Published by Running Press, an imprint of Hachette Book Group, Inc.
The Running Press name and logo are trademarks of Hachette Book Group, Inc.

The Hachette Speakers Bureau provides a wide range of authors for speaking events. To find out more, go to www.hachettespeakersbureau.com or email HachetteSpeakers@hbgusa.com.

Running Press books may be purchased in bulk for business, educational, or promotional use. For more information, please contact your local bookseller or the Hachette Book Group Special Markets Department at Special.Markets@hbgusa.com.

The publisher is not responsible for websites (or their content) that are not owned by the publisher.

Print book cover and interior design by Tanvi Baghele

Library of Congress Control Number: 2024933955

ISBNs: 978-0-7624-8839-1 (hardcover), 978-0-7624-8840-7 (ebook)

Printed in China

APS

10 9 8 7 6 5 4 3 2 1

LIFE IS BETTER WITH

PEEPS®

Please. If there's one thing we can all agree on, let it be PEEPS®. In a world full of shame, sorrow, and chaos, these cheerful and free-spirited marshmallow treats just want to be loved—and eaten. If you've never had PEEPS® Marshmallow, then what are you actually doing with your life? PEEPS® are sparkle-coated, sweet treats of pure happiness. They taste like magical marshmallows and little globs of goodness. Plus, they're cute. Can you honestly look a PEEPS® Chick or Bunny in the face with those little, brown eyes and not feel all warm and fuzzy? On a dark, cloudy day, PEEPS® are like a small spot of sunshine. When life is hard and nothing seems to be going your way, PEEPS® are there for you. All PEEPS® want is to make you happy. For Peep's sake—if loving PEEPS® is wrong, then I sure as sugar don't want to be right. Thank heavens for PEEPS®.

Hangin' with my Peeps

Holla
at my Peeps

Party Peeps

Peeps down

Not your average Peeps

Have your Peeps call my Peeps

Two Peeps
in a pod

Sweet and
I know it

V-I-PEEPS

Power to
the Peeps

All we are saying is give Peeps a chance

Hide and go Peeps

One
tough Chick

Where my Peeps at?

Peeps on Earth

Peeps run
this place

Two cool Peeps

Express your
PEEPSONALITY®

Peepin' it real

That sweet Peeps life

Peeps magnet

Peeps
stick together

Long live Peeps

Trick or Peeps

Hot
Peeps summer

Peeps for your thoughts

Peeps of a feather

Two Peeps are better than one

Peeps on fleek

Live, laugh, Peeps

Eat. Peeps. Sleep. Repeat.

Peeps just wanna have fun

Peeps is my superpower

Peeps, but make it fabulous

Peeps
game strong

Peeps state of mind

Get your Peeps on

The future is Peeps